WHEN THE A A MAN SALUTED

MORE HALCYON DAYS OF MOTORING

A.B. DEMAUS

SUTTON PUBLISHING

First published in the United Kingdom in 2008 by
Sutton Publishing, an imprint of NPI Media Group Limited
Cirencester Road · Chalford · Stroud · Gloucestershire · GL6 8PE

British Library Cataloguing in Publication Data
A catalogue record for this book is available from the British Library.

ISBN 978-0-7509-4857-9

Typeset in 10.5/13.5 Photina
Typesetting and origination by
NPI Media Group Limited.
Printed and bound in England.

Contents

Acknowledgements

The author gratefully acknowledges the generous help he has received over many years from a host of friends and fellow enthusiasts in the collecting of his photographic archive. Individual photographs are each acknowledged separately. Where no such acknowledgement appears, the photograph had no attribution when acquired and has defied further research. Inevitably there will be some omissions for which sincere apologies are offered.

Reunion after fifty years! The author (right) with the present owner of the 14/60 Lagonda formerly in the author's ownership, that had been lost to ken for seventeen years. *(C. Lunt)*

Introduction

Let us forget motorways and just imagine our favourite road in the British Isles – anywhere in the British Isles. Every reader will have a particular choice, be it in a high-banked sweet-scented West Country lane, a windswept track bounded by dry-stone walls in the higher regions of the Cotswolds, a steeply-graded and tortuous road in the Scottish Highlands, or what you will. It may have been marched over by Roman legions or echoed to the tramp of the military in other turbulent times.

However, one thing is certain and that is that it will have seen more change in the last 120 years or so than at any other time in its history. Why? Because of the coming of the motor car, let loose on the roads of Britain after The Locomotives on Highways Act of 1896.

Such a minute fragment of history, 120 years! But a fragment packed with the history and development of the motor car itself. The motor car has now reached a point where the damage it does to the environment is beginning to outweigh the very advantages that its invention and use brought about.

By means of very carefully selected photographs, this book is an attempt to turn the spotlight on the first forty years or so – 1900 to 1940. Look at more than the cars and motorcycles, look at their riders or drivers, their passengers, the people in general, the fashions in clothing and street furniture and the many little items that a casual glance may so easily miss, and be grateful that the photographer, amateur or professional, captured that fleeting moment in time to the best of his or her ability.

A.B. Demaus
January 2008

The chauffeur sits proudly at the wheel of his employer's fine 16/20 Beeston Humber when it was brand new on 1 March 1906. It was registered to John Charles Harford, Falcondale, Lampeter, as EJ 26. It was coloured dark blue.

Brooklands Guy's Hospital Gala Day, 2 July 1932. One of the Humbers (1930 model) that brought the Duke and Duchess of York to the event bears the scrutiny of a bowler-hatted gentleman. Beside him stand the two chauffeurs. *(The Humber Register)*

1

The Formative Years to 1918

This is an 1899 'vis-à-vis', Star's first venture into motor manufacture. It was closely based on the Benz and is seen here with Thomas Gibbons and Edward Lisle at Hill Top, West Bromwich. *(P. Gibbons)*

The 3hp Léon Bollée voiturette appeared in 1895, though as a pioneer motorist you would probably have progressed to something more up-to-date by 1900. They were produced in quite large numbers, some even made under licence in Britain. This example is in pristine condition. *(H.J.F. Thompson)*

This impressive Panhard & Levassor was supplied to the Bishop of Worcester, *c.* 1902. It boasts a magnificent set of lamps. *(Worcester RO)*

Pictured as it is just about to set out on another day of a Scottish tour undertaken in 1902 is this Panhard & Levassor. *(Mrs Scott)*

South Wales, 1903. Bert Yates, wearing a splendid jersey with the Humber CC logo, and Humber racer. He had successes at Carmarthen and Pontypridd that year. *(Lynn Hughes)*

The MCC Inter-Team Trial at Bicester in 1904 reveals Humber, Excelsior, Triumph and Riley machines with, from left to right, Sam Wright, Bert Yates, R.W. Ayton, H.W. Duret, B.H. Owen and Alan Riley. *(R. Howard)*

From the very earliest days of motoring, manufacturers sought to bring their products to the attention of the public through competition success. Here is one of the two Mobile cars that took part in the Small Car Trials in Hereford in 1904. Note the early form of trade plate, the 'O' indicating Birmingham where the cars were made and 'ME', the first and last letters of their name.

The animated scene in High Street, Hereford, during the 1904 Small Car Trials. Dorothy Levitt was a versatile and accomplished driver and very popular with the RAC observers like the young man beside her. *(B. Butcher)*

This well-laden Wolseley rear-entrance wagonette is seen in the Herefordshire countryside, *c.* 1904. The driver is standing beside the near-side front wheel. *(Pritchard, Hereford)*

Numerous small firms embarked on motorcycle manufacture in the pioneering years. Here is one made by Arthur Williams of Glanamman, Carmarthenshire, makers of Defiance cycles, registered BX19 on 7 June 1904. *(Lynn Hughes)*

This big V-twin Rex dates from 1905 and seems in fine order. Its rider also displays sartorial elegance unusual for a motorcyclist!

Seen here on the Clee Hills near Ludlow is a Riley forecar and a Royal Severn motorcycle, Reg. No. AB 184, new on 29 January 1904. Its engine was made by the Noble Manufacturing Co. It was owned in Kidderminster. (*The Midland Automobile Club*)

This Decauville (0–87) is seen on an Easter tour of North Wales undertaken in 1905 and is pictured here between Llyn Ogwen and Bethesda. (*The Midland Automobile Club*)

A 6hp Quadrant tri-car first registered as AR 717 on 20 February 1905 to an owner near Ware, Hertfordshire. Quite what role the military may be concerned with is open to question.

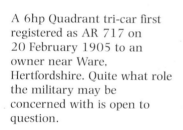

Decauville 0–87 was a much-travelled car. At Easter 1906 its Kidderminster owner embarked upon a motor tour to the Lake District. Here they start from Wakefield on the second day of the tour. (*The Midland Automobile Club*)

Easter came early that year and this lunchtime picnic near Doncaster would appear to be quite a spartan affair with no leaves on the trees. (*The Midland Automobile Club*)

This unidentified machine may predate 1 January 1904, or maybe it is too new to have been registered. It is seen here outside the Clarke Robinson depot at Barnham, where banking hours seem minimal! (*H.J.F. Thompson*)

A winter scene in Lincolnshire at Christmas 1906, as this Argyll-registered FE 265 takes to the snow. (*Capt. J. Aston, RN*)

This is one of Raphael Tuck's 'Oilette' series and is captioned 'Motoring – A good run'. It portrays a medium-sized touring car of about 1907. . .

. . . its companion is captioned 'Breaking the Record', obviously on a sandy beach somewhere. One wonders why the two passengers in the rear were there during a record attempt.

Fromes Hill, near Ledbury, May 1907. This event was very well attended, but No. 67 appears to be very reluctant to start . . .

. . . but there are plenty of willing helpers available to push. (*T. Ward*)

This 20hp Richard-Brasier with its white-coated chauffeur was photographed in August 1905 . . .

. . . and this front view reveals it as being registered LC 1609, a London registration. These cars were made by the Société des Anciens Etablissements Georges Richard at Ivry-Port. (*R.J.R. Benson*)

Mr Marriott of Hereford, who owned a garage business from the very early days, is seen here with a Vulcan car, registered FY 84 (Southport Borough), a make for which he held the agency. *(A.W. Marriott)*

Here is a 16/20 Sunbeam registered in Shropshire as AW 79, with Mrs Thursby at the wheel and the chauffeur on the far right. This photograph was taken at Orleton, Wellington, Shropshire. *(R.J.R. Benson)*

This Darracq bears a Cardiff registration number. For a family car of this size it is surprisingly devoid of weather equipment, with no windscreen or hood.

This imposing 30hp Beeston-Humber of 1907 is well laden. The mounting of a bulb horn on the passenger side is perhaps a little unusual. *(M. McCutcheon)*

W. & G. du Cros Ltd was founded by two members of the du Cros family who were pioneers in the motor trade. Seen here is their works at Acton Vale, London, where their large fleet of 2-cylinder cabs was maintained.

A Daimler dating from about 1908 stands outside the door of Lower Eaton Court, near Hereford. The flags may indicate the year is 1910 and King George V's accession is being celebrated. (*Bustin, Hereford*)

Two splendid shots of a 20/30hp Renault, single phaeton with leather hood, dark green, registered new as EI 117 (County Sligo) on 31 August 1909 to Capt. Stanley Paddon, 10 Cadogan Mansions, Sloane Square, London . . .

. . . the huge headlamps are very impressive and probably mounted high on the mudguards because Renault bonnets hinged from the back and lifted upwards. *(S. Hall)*

All the ingredients for a picnic of the time are contained in this shot of a family with their 1910 12hp Humber – a pleasant spot in the country, sun and shade, and what would seem to be an ample repast. The car was registered AB 1542 on 17 June 1910, and was finished in Humber green. *(The Humber Register)*

It may surprise some that even quite minor British makes ventured in to Continental competition before 1914. Calthorpes were made by the Calthorpe Motor Co., Birmingham. This example of one of their racing cars was driven by Weidman in the Coupe des Voiturettes in 1909. He seems, with his pipe in his mouth, to be very relaxed about the competition. *(B. Mills)*

Seen approaching Ross-on-Wye is this 15hp Austin single landaulette painted lake and red, registered as CJ 696 on 4 April 1910 to Lady Lucy Fitzmayer of Lower Weston. *('Herefordshire Lore')*

The Unic was made in France but this name was very familiar in this country because from 1908 their 4-cylinder model was in very wide use as a taxi, particularly in London, right up to the early 1930s. Here is their 4.1-litre model with an Essex registration (F), pictured on a misty winter day.

This Clement-Talbot carries a Herefordshire registration of CJ 845. It was supplied new to William H. Lawton of Colwall on 6 March 1911. Later it became the property of Miss Ada Lamb, also of Colwall.

A 10hp open Delage with the Shropshire registration AW 560 is the sole motor vehicle in High Street, Market Drayton, on this occasion. It can't have been market day!

The inaugural meeting of the Redditch & DMCC, May 1910. This club had many keen and active members and supported many competition events. *(F.W. Viles)*

This young man may perhaps have used his smart new Premier motorcycle to influence his two charming ladies to a trip in the country. *(R. Howard)*

Lincoln Elk motorcycles were made by J. Kirby, Broadgate, Lincoln, from 1902 to 1924. Before 1914 they concentrated on s.v. single-cylinder engines of 402cc and 499cc of their own make. This machine dates from about 1912.

Here is Bert Bladder of Worcester astride a pristine Rudge on trade plates. He became a well-known and successful competition rider. (*M. Dowty*)

This seems rather a casual way to try to repair a punctured rear tyre on a motorcycle, but hopefully it all went together again.
(R.J.R. Benson)

As well as making engines widely available to other manufacturers, Minerva were very early in the business of making and selling Minerva machines to the public. This example wears a Leeds registration.
(D. Foxton)

This rather serious young man is astride an NSU, a German make from Neckarsulm where they made a very wide range of models, in the early years favouring an inlet-over-exhaust layout. This one carries a London registration.

Wicker sidecars were attractive to look at and light in weight, hence their popularity. This is a trade card by one of their most prominent makers and dates from 1911.

Bert Yates was a well-known works rider for Humber Ltd, and is seen here on Rest-and-be-Thankful, a formidable Scottish trials hill, in 1910. (*L.K. Tavinor*)

We have met Rudge FKC-2 (a Worcester City trade plate) before. Now this young man is joined by a fellow enthusiast who rides a Worcester City-registered (FK 278) Bradbury machine. *(Worcester RO)*

This well-equipped Clyno combination stands in an almost deserted street to pose for the camera. Note the wicker sidecar beneath the tarpaulin. The registration is a Northampton one. *(P. Klein)*

All hands stop work for the photographer, but once the lens is out of the way this Humber Ltd workshop will again hum with activity. The picture dates from about 1912 and open cars still predominate. (*The Humber Register*)

Remarkably similar in appearance to the much better-known Napier, this is a 60hp Thames built by Thames Iron Works who were also builders of battleships!

From *The Autocar* 3 February 1912: 'A Humber Ambulance Car supplied by Messrs Holl and Bros. of Boston Road, Sleaford, to the Sleaford Hospital authorities. The car runs on Lynton wheels and tyres so far as the back is concerned, and has been doing so since last October.'

Two Coventry-built Siddeley-Deasys on trade plates are seen here at a refreshment halt at the King's Arms. They carry simple test-rig bodywork. Such test trips into the countryside were a handy way to combine business and pleasure.

Part of a large stable of cars of the Edwardian period. The child at the wheel of the Panhard et Levassor (AA 8648) is a pleasant touch and almost everybody has got in on the act. This estate must have employed a large staff.

The esplanade and gardens at Ryde are quiet on this sunny morning apart from horse-drawn and motor hire vehicles.

Automobiles H. Demeester, Courbevoie, Seine, were the makers of this car. In existence from 1906 to 1914, the company was quite active in voiturette racing.

The 3-wheeler AC 'Sociable' was one of the more unusual designs to emanate from the works of Autocarriers (1911) Ltd., Thames Ditton, Surrey. Single-cylindered and with a rear-mounted engine, they were tiller-steered.

A smartly uniformed servant has the travelling rug handy for milady to step into this superbly elegant sleeve-valve Daimler of about 1913.

The major Scottish firm of Arrol-Johnston produced some fine cars of which this is an example. Note the radiator behind the engine, à la Renault, and the quick-detachable artillery wheels. This firm, like its Scottish sister the Argyll, was one of the few to fit fwb before 1914. Arrol-Johnston were not happy with the result and discontinued the practice.

One presumes that the children seen on the right belonged with this tall, electrically-lit Wolseley landaulette. One wouldn't stop in such a place for a photo-call these days!

This young man and his lady pose in a C.I.D. 'Baby' cyclecar: 8hp single-cylinder Buchet engine and 4-speed friction transmission. They were built in Dijon from 1912–14. The backdrop is a typical photographer's studio effort.

A large Metallurgique with a Carmarthenshire registration is here being used to transport two motorcycles – one on each running-board – to a motorcycle competition. *(Lynn Hughes)*

A better-known cyclecar was the air-cooled two-cylinder Humberette of late 1913, seen here in the shade of Dunster's village street beneath the castle.

A fine example of a 2-cylinder Swift 10hp shaft-drive light car. It made an ideal ladies' car: light, manoeuvrable and economical. *(Lynn Hughes)*

This rare light car dating from 1913 is an Averies, made at Englefield Green, Surrey, by Averies-Ponette Ltd. It bore a Surrey registration of PA 5012, but is seen here in Shropshire, its owner's home county. *(R.J.R. Benson)*

A much-travelled 1914 10hp Humber is out and about again for yet another picnic in which there seems to be no shortage of picnic gear.

Still in small car mode, the 2-cylinder Humberette had a very similar specification. Offered at first with air-cooling, as here, a water-cooled option became available for 1914. These cars were made in much greater numbers than the Swift in the previous picture. Note the warning to cyclists. (*The Humber Register*)

Another make with a broadly similar specification was the Perry, but water-cooled this time. This 2-cylinder model became the forerunner of the Bean and was made in Birmingham from where its 'OA' registration comes. (*B.K. Goodman*)

Roy (later Sir Roy) Fedden was the inspiration for the sporting 4-cylinder 3-litre 15hp Straker-Squire, a car of excellent quality and performance. The low, sleek lines of this example are an indication of its appeal. *(R. Cookson)*

The animated scene at Chipping Norton, Oxfordshire, as competitors assemble for the MCC Inter-Team Trials, 1913.

This generation rides a very business-like Belgian F.N. shaft-drive 4-cylinder machine, well-equipped with accessories including two headlights, acetylene gas generator, two-note bulb horn and a rear-view mirror. *(G.D. Smith)*

A water-cooled Williamson combination is seen here participating in a trial, *c.* 1912. The 996cc engines for this make were made by Douglas Motors Ltd, of Bristol.

At the same location on the same trial as the picture at the bottom of page 45 we see an interesting batch of machines. Here we see a smart P&M in the foreground and behind it a round-tanked B.A.T. (Best After Tests) may be picked out.

The Stevens daughters, Ethel on the left, flank a single male as part of a Stevens family photograph, *c.* 1913 . . .

. . . while 'paterfamilias' rides in comfort in a big V-twin AJS adapted to be steered from the sidecar.
(Mrs E. Simpson)

This rider with a machine registered in Norwich pulls over to consult the very clear signpost.

Young lads put their machine to the test against the steep gradient of Town Hill, Swansea, *c.* 1913. The elderly lady on the pavement looks decidedly disapproving! *(Lynn Hughes)*

T.G. Knowles with his impeccably presented round-tank 2¾hp TT Humber V-twin, 1913. He finished in 11th place with a time of 6h. 7m. 58s. in the Junior TT. *(Miss M. Burgess)*

George Dance with Sunbeam and AJS test riders gather in the countryside near Wolverhampton, 1915. In the background is a Briton car, also made in Wolverhampton. (*F.W. Giles*)

Opposite: These two Model-T Fords, suitably adapted, were participants in an event that, in the words of the contemporary press, 'attracted all social London'. This was the first ever motor polo match held at Ranelagh on 31 May 1913.

The series of motor races termed the Tourist Trophy (TT) were inaugurated in the Isle of Man in 1905. The first year in which it became a true race for out-and-out racing cars (but limited to a cylinder bore of 4in) was 1908, when the Belgian Oscar Cupper contrived to invert his Metallurgique in practice. *(S. Hall)*

The speed hill-climb at Caerphilly in 1913. W.G. Tuck's sprint Humber raises the dust as he corners. *(The Humber Register)*

British cars and drivers were active on the Continent also in 1913, in which year both Sunbeams and Vauxhalls competed in the Coupe de l'Auto on the Boulogne circuit. Here is the Sunbeam of Kenelm Lee Guinness at the start . . .

. . . and the Vauxhall of W. Watson on the course which is lined by some not-too-substantial barriers to keep back the eager spectators.

The sands at Porthcawl were a site for sand racing before the First World War. Here, in 1914, a Clement-Talbot entered by the Earl of Shrewsbury climbs the wooden ramp provided to enable cars to go from the sands to the spectators' area. *(A.R. Abbott)*

Many enquiries have failed to identify this very purposeful-looking sports-racing car. It has very rakish **lines** and the front-axle has been liberally drilled. The unusual dashboard is well instrumented and all **surplus** material dispensed with. *(J. Pratt)*

This commodius 25/30hp Alldays of 1914 is very fully equipped with an Auster folding screen for the rear compartment and the folded hood neatly encased in a hood bag. It carries a Wolverhampton (DA) registration.

The team of sleeve-valve Minervas that entered for the 1914 Tourist Trophy poured out generous volumes of oily smoke which led to complaints. The race officials carried out some tests in the hope of quelling the complaints, but it made no difference, as witnessed by Riecken's Minerva III. *(Worcester RO)*

Two Wolverhampton-built Star cars were entered for the race. Various troubles dogged them in practice and in the race both retired after five laps. *(Miss M. Burgess)*

Shortly after the TT, the threat of war loomed ever more menacingly and became a reality in August 1914. Here one of the huge number of Crossley staff cars that were pressed into service is seen somewhere in the Middle East. *(Pritchard, Hereford)*

This Model-T Ford ambulance with its driver and nursing orderly are photographed here immediately before embarkation for Salonika.

A Crossley ambulance is joined by two Model-T Fords and a Wolseley. Military personnel with this unit include three ladies.

These soldiers have obtained the use of an elderly Argyll that was supplied new to E. Henry, Charlton **House**, Tetbury, Gloucestershire, on 17 March 1905 and registered as AD 458. They don't seem to be **treating** it considerately!

One of the beautiful 9-cylinder radial engines designed by W.O. Bentley and made in the Coventry works of Humber Ltd, among others, is seen here with Royal Naval Air Service personnel beside it. (N.W. Portway)

A Royal Navy captain and a military officer stand beside this Morris Oxford two-seater with its lady occupants at Longhope, near Scapa Flow in the Orkneys, 1915. *(Capt. J. Aston, RN)*

The driver and five passengers fit comfortably in this tourer, photographed in July 1917. The driver's white coat probably indicates he is a professional and it is a hire car.

This unidentified American car has been painstakingly decorated, in somewhat garish taste, perhaps, for an Armistice parade, 1918. *(National Library of Wales)*

Mr Pritchett with his smart Standard light car waves goodbye to us – and to greet the vastly changed world of post-1918, perhaps? *(H.S. Humphrey)*

2

Post 1918

The small boy in this Panhard et Levassor, registered in Wolverhampton as DA 1479 in 1921,
looks eager to embrace the 'brave new world' that was promised after the Armistice.

This young lad proudly seated behind the wheel of his parents' pre-war Morris Oxford (in beautiful order) is of school age. Note the mounting of the speedometer drive by cable from the off-side front wheel. His mother stands proudly by. *(R. Judd)*

A slightly later Morris Oxford with a BW (Oxfordshire) registration takes this cheerful party and a motorcycling friend out into its home county.

A 6-cylinder 24/30hp Wolseley, with the registration CC 2819. It had the chassis no. M8 No. 11, the engine no. 13A/2505, and was first registered in 1920. The other details of the vehicle are as follows: Weight: 33 cwts. Originally tourer, dark blue. Colour change to grey (1924). Registered as Hackney 6 August 1925. Change of ownership 22 March 1927. Changed to saloon body, colour khaki 2 March 1928. Owner: Thomas Owen, The Oxford Garage, Somerset Street, Llandudno.

In the background is a large open Wolseley which dwarfs the little 8/18 Humber (unusually on balloon tyres) in front of it. Sadly in this instance the location is unknown. *(P. Diffey)*

Catch 'em young! Sandwiched between two GNs, the one on the right belonging to 'Archie' Frazer Nash, is Trubie Moore's son in a chain-drive pedal car with 'Archie' himself behind it. *(Mrs G. Moore)*

A young boy in a Triang pedal car snapped on the promenade of a large seaside resort. His pal prefers a trike.

At what is probably a northern location, a Calcott drophead coupé wears what appears to be a very large bushy-tailed black cat mascot, a popular subject in the early 1920s.

1920s touring cars were roomy. If, as in this case, an Auster folding rear screen was fitted, it made an admirable picnic table when folded flat. This party of cheerful ladies and a small child enjoy an alfresco meal in a 1920 inlet-over-exhaust valve 18hp Essex-registered DW 1965 (Newport, Monmouth) owned at the time by a Mr Rosser who probably took the photograph. (*W.G. Rosser*)

These three elderly picnickers were using the main part of the car's Auster screen in a similar fashion.

A Humber official photograph from 1922 shows six sv 11hp models: four four-seater tourers, one coupé and a 2-seater tourer. The leading three cars carry consecutive (CM Birkenhead) registrations, while the fourth four-seater is on trade plates. Note that on all the open models the door handles point vertically downwards in the closed position and are pulled upwards to open. This cleverly obviates the accidental opening of the door by leaning on the handle or by force of gravity. *(The Humber Register)*

This very pretty little polished aluminium-bodied sports model on an Austin Seven chassis is a Gordon England 'Rudge-Whitworth' model, a much rarer bird than the 'Brooklands' model. Note the fairings around the stub axles. *(E. Widgery)*

The ladies gather round a smart Douglas flat-twin combination with polished aluminium wheel discs. A Harley-Davidson brings up the rear, together with an unidentified machine, in west Herefordshire, *c.* 1921. *(Pritchard, Hereford)*

As with cars, the Americans were much quicker to make use of electric lighting on motorcycles than we were. This big Harley-Davidson combination also boasts disc wheels – easy to keep clean but sometimes risky in side winds. *(Pritchard, Hereford)*

A trade card for the Ner-a-car, an unusual machine designed by an American, J. Neracher, to try to combat the bugbears of the need for protective clothing against the elements and road dirt. Note the generous mudguarding and low seating position. Whether the name is a play on 'Near-a-car' or the designer's name is open to question.

Handel Davies with his 3hp ABC on the Cuckoo Bend in the Black Mountain Open hill-climb in the wild scenery of Wales on 8 September 1921. *(Lynn Hughes)*

The Triumph riders for the 1921 Senior TT race. They are, from left to right: C. Sgonina, S. Gill, G.J. Sherman and H. Pattinson. Sgonina, as usual, sports a white polo-neck sweater. *(Mrs C. Sgonina)*

Seen here is the AJS on which Cyril Williams won the 1920 Junior TT in the Isle of Man. It shows every sign of having weathered a hard race. By contrast, the three Isle of Man visitors relax in smart suits and hats. *(Mrs C. Sgonina)*

Silverware – the rewards of success. Reg Brown of Hereford, where he ran a garage business, with his Gloucestershire-registered Sunbeam AD 266. *(Bustin, Hereford)*

A motorcycle grass track event in the mid-1920s. The two machines on the right, nearest the starter, are Cottons, made in Gloucester.

Prince Albert, later King George VI, with a fine Douglas flat-twin. Note the maker's characteristic disc brake on the front wheel – vastly more effective than the usual stirrup brake acting on the rim of the wheel. (*M. Dowty*)

It is seldom realised that Kaye Don competed at home and abroad as a motorcyclist long before he made his name with cars and as a record-breaker. Here he is seen at the International hill-climb at Liège on 7 May 1922 with his 499cc Norton.

An Excelsior on trade plates taking part in the Colmore Cup Trial on 24 February 1923. There would have been very many more spectators on the more testing parts of the route. *(F.R. Logan)*

The patrolmen of the AA or RAC were often on hand to smooth the motorists' path. Here an AA man gives advice, probably navigational, to lady motorists with their Standard in the West Country.

The Crossley 20/70 was a sporting development of the 19.6hp touring car. A well-engineered quality production but still of Edwardian conception. This car is being road tested by A. Symonds near Sidmouth, Devon, at Easter, 1924.

The Sizaire-Berwick was an Anglo-French car of even higher quality and always of handsome appearance. A novel feature was that the whole of the instrument panel could be hinged outwards to give clear access to the electrical wiring and instruments. (N. Bell)

GNs, with their lightweight and sporting performance with economy, were firm favourites with sporty motorists of limited means. Here is a gaggle of them spectating at Sutton Bank hill-climb, Yorkshire, 1921. *(Mrs G. Moore)*

Typical of the state of minor roads in rural areas in winter is this sea of mud and ruts. The Bayliss-Thomas struggling here bears a competition number (8), so is likely to be taking part in a trial, *c.* 1923.

Captain Mark-Wardlaw RN is seen here at the wheel of his neat new Wolseley 10hp of about 1922. These small Wolseleys boasted an ohc-engine derived from the firm's aero-engine experience in the war. (*Capt. J. Aston RN*)

The spectacular Forth Bridge was often chosen as a backdrop for photographers. Here we see one of Lionel Martin's early Aston Martin racing-cars when in private ownership. *(J. Martin)*

A car is invaluable at the time of a general election and here we see Stanley Baldwin canvassing in Worcestershire at such a time. The car is a 23/60 Vauxhall. *(P. Hingston)*

A famous engineer and racing driver of the early 1920s, Clive Gallop, is seen at the wheel of his sporting G.N. The male passenger is Michael Haworth-Booth and the cat seems almost supernumerary. *(M. Haworth-Booth)*

A charity parade of Crouch cars. The placards on the cars read 'The Crouch car is the First Prize in the great motor ballot in aid of funds for the Coventry & N. Warwickshire Hospital.' Note the absence of lights on the majority of cars, probably assembled in a hurry.

A splendid shot of Gordon England's trademark on the wall plaques. GE bodies usually carried a miniature version on the scuttle sides low down near the valance. Business houses such as pharmaceutical suppliers tended to favour the staid and gentlemanly image of the Armstrong-Siddeley for their travelling salesmen and doubtless this batch of three went to the same customer. *(E. Widgery)*

An early Bullnose Morris with aluminium disc wheels (note the spare) and a Rover 9/20 sports in polished aluminium are posed in front of a country house. The gentleman beside the Rover is probably the car's owner, *c.* 1927.

These two pictures of an Austin 20hp landaulette and a Morris Oxford Six demonstrate the robust usefulness of vintage running-boards.

This 1930 Morris Oxford Six has running-boards amply roomy enough for the driver, four rather bulky ladies and the pet dog.

It is quite common to find that the family's pet dog takes a delight in motoring. This one sits proudly a-top his master's Deemster. *(Mrs G. Moore)*

Here is G.S. Boston in his newly acquired 1½-litre 'Sascha' Austro-Daimler, ex-Malcolm Campbell. When Boston competed with it, it was repainted in dark blue with red wheels. The dog seems to be about to make a rapid exit! *(G.S. Boston)*

The 4-cylinder 11.9hp Mercury was an entirely orthodox British car made in small numbers by Mercury Cars (Production) Ltd, of Twickenham, Middlesex.

The ladies in this 8hp Gwynne have used a trip into the country to gather bunches of wild flowers – a practice that would be frowned upon today.

The esplanade, new pier and pavilion at Penarth, South Wales, are sunny and bright on this summer day in about 1930. Two cars, a Bullnose Morris in the far distance and a Middlesex-registered Morris Oxford saloon in the foreground, a motorcycle and a pedal cycle are the only vehicles to be seen.

A 10/23 Talbot (left) and a Scripps-Booth first registered in Kingston-upon-Hull on 17 November 1919 and painted maroon, lined crimson are seen in this snap dating from about 1927. *(Mrs G. Moore)*

Opposite: A fine sporting 2LS Ballot driven by Henry Spurrier, of Leyland fame, copes with the appallingly rough Lake District passes where the car seems quite dwarfed by the rugged scenery. *(Mrs P. Perrin)*

Here is Charlie Sgonina, Welsh motorcycling ace, sitting on the running board of the 1914 TT Humber he acquired shortly after the Armistice. He is at an unidentified speed event in South Wales. By the greatest good fortune this car survives and competes regularly in vintage speed events. It is the only known survivor. *(Mrs C. Sgonina)*

Lionel Rapson made record attempts to advertise his Rapson tyres. He is seen here in August 1924 in the driving seat of his special Lanchester. Duller is on the off side, wearing a helmet in this bid for the 12-hour record. *(C. Donovan)*

The 1922 ex-Zborowski Aston Martin that became 'Green Pea' in the ownership of Marion Agnew and Robert Morgan in a new guise as a 'Thomas Speciale' (on account of its Hooker-Thomas engine) in the 1925 Boulogne GP. Marion Agnew stands beside the driver's seat and Robert Morgan on the near side. They finished in third place overall. (*Ferret Photos*)

Brooklands again as H.V. Barlow in the big 21, 504cc chain-drive Benz attracts a crowd in August 1922. *(W. Gibbs)*

Opposite: Great things were expected of the two Italian Fiats entered for the 1923 200-Miles Race at Brooklands, to be driven by Malcolm Campbell and Charles Salamano, but they both retired. *(G.S. Boston)*

The 200-Miles Race, 1921, presents a scene full of activity as competing cars leave the start. Prominent in the foreground are no. 31, Bugatti with Hillman (25), Enfield-Allday (26), Horstman (27), Alvis (28) and Charron-Laycock (29). This event, inaugurated in 1921 by the JCC (Junior Car Club), became a classic and always attracted a keen and competitive entry.

A pleasing group, left to right, of a Gordon England 'Cup' model Austin Seven sporting polished aluminium wheel discs, a 14/40 Sunbeam saloon and two 2-seater Alvis cars . . .

. . . with here, in close-up, one of the latter, this time with the hood up.

Off for Christmas! Driver and passenger are about to embark – the passenger's door is open – in this well-laden Vauxhall 30/98. Despite the obviously wintry weather, no attempt has been made to erect the hood which is still neatly furled in its hoodbag. Some warming Christmas cheer will be in order on arrival, no doubt! *(G.S. Boston)*

The 15.9hp Hotchkiss was a medium-powered quality car from France. Here we see open and closed coachwork on this chassis; both are handsome. TW is an Essex registration, YF a London one.

A Palladium in company with a 20hp Vulcan landaulette and a Bullnose Morris pays a call at Castle Howard, Yorkshire. *(Mrs G. Moore)*

A close-up of the smart and pleasantly proportioned sports body on a 11.9hp Anzani-engined Crouch.

A handsome Delage tourer stops to allow its occupants to stretch their legs. Note the toolboxes above and below the running board and the fibre stepmat in its frame for the benefit of the rear passengers.

Continental makers did not favour the folding rear screen so typical of many British touring cars. A popular alternative was the rear cowl and screen or screens, as on this 12hp Darracq of about 1925. (*Mrs G. Moore*)

This elderly gentleman looks quite contented to be sitting in a Shropshire-registered Talbot 10/23 in a rural lane in that county as he smokes his pipe.

The original caption to this picture is: 'Slow running weak!' The car is a fine 30/98 Vauxhall which made an extensive Continental tour in the 1920s. The car is on the left of the road which, together with the background, suggests this adjustment (note the cigarette!) is on British soil. *(G. Summers)*

On the Continent this time as the car is snapped at a lunch stop on the Stelvio Pass. *(G. Summers)*

A 3-litre Bentley and a 30/98 Vauxhall pay a compulsory call at Austrian customs while touring on the Continent in the mid-1920s. *(G. Summers)*

This Worcestershire-registered 18hp Essex tourer was a much-travelled car, covering considerable miles in this country and abroad. It is seen here during a Swiss tour.

The Vauxhall 30/98 is snapped again on the same tour, this time on the Pordoi Pass. *(G. Summers)*

A year later this Vauxhall 30/98 is pictured while driver and passenger take a roadside break near Bad Ems. (*G. Summers*)

In 1931 Lionel Martin with two passengers took a new Hillman Wizard on an extensive and punishing Continental tour in the course of which they climbed sixteen passes of over 7,000ft in altitude and covered 2,500 miles. Here we see, from left to right: John Martin, Lionel Martin and Henry Gadsby with the car at the summit of the Stelvio Pass. *(John Martin)*

Not what it seems, as this is not real trouble. It is a posed shot, most probably for a motoring periodical, demonstrating care and maintenance of a Singer car. *(J. Pratt)*

Opposite: A Brocklebank Six saloon featured against the lighthouse at Mull of Galloway, Easter 1927. The Brocklebank was a very orthodox car that did not enjoy a great success. *(Mrs G. Moore)*

This 3-litre Van den Plas Bentley speed model is seen near Southborough, Kent. It was succeeded in the same ownership by . . .

. . . a shapely but massive 6½-litre fixed-head coupé with coachwork by Park Ward. (*J.D. Leathley*)

Before the days of potted palms or dolly birds we see the Humber Show stand in 1926. On the left is the newly introduced 9/20 in tourer guise and on the right of it a 15/40 tourer. In the background is a 9/20 saloon and part views of a 12/25 and 15/40 saloon. *(A. Ingram/The Humber Register)*

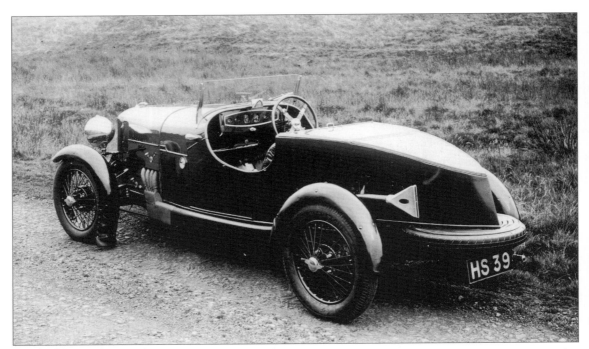

This is but one of a series of specials using Humber components that a Scottish firm turned out. See also page 117 (bottom). *(The Humber Register)*

A very varied stable of vintage cars owned by a Shropshire enthusiast. From left to right they are an Avon-bodied Austin Seven, a potent single-seater GN and a 24hp Sunbeam sporting model. The Sunbeam was registered CJ 2983 on 3 February 1921. It was finished in red with a polished aluminium bonnet. *(J. Hall)*

Thompson & Taylor's Weybridge works where, after Parry Thomas's death at Pendine, his former assistant Reid Railton ministered to many racing and record-breaking cars. Here we see an exciting line-up with some of the personnel. *(C. Cottrell)*

The engine shop of a very small provincial manufacturer who produced the Castle-Three in Kidderminster, Worcestershire. Chassis nos 106 onwards in sequence, from left to right. Bill Lewis, in the white overalls, is the overseer.

This Herefordshire-registered Bullnose Morris two-seater has met with a roadside mishap. The damage doesn't seem too serious and will doubtless be repaired when the car can be taken to the local garage. (*F. Williams*)

Here is the impressive showroom of the Castle Motor Company Limited in Kidderminster, Worcestershire. Examples of Renault, Essex and Bullnose Morris may be seen among others.

One of the most popular Austin Seven models was the Gordon England 'Cup' model which was attractively proportioned. Here in the Gordon England Works is an array of 'Cup' models with some standard 'chummies' on the right. *(E. Widgery)*

Here is a typical village garage in a rural county, in this case Herefordshire. Business seems slack at the time of this shot. The building remains unaltered today. *(R.A. Bird)*

The lengthy double-decker car transporter familiar now was a long way into the future when this Riley Nine was driven from the factory to the agent in 1930. A contrast, too, with the manners of today! (*A.R. Abbott*)

Two lady motorcyclists (who probably just posed for the photograph) outside One Shop Cottage, Leintwardine, Herefordshire, c. 1920. (*Leintwardine Local History Society*)

The firm of Anderson of Newton Mearns, Renfrewshire, were old-established Humber agents with extensive engineering facilities. This 'special' used 9/28 Humber components. The advanced thinking in the clever use of 'space frame' construction should be noted. The complete car was very good-looking and may be seen at the top of page 112. (*The Humber Register*)

British motorcyclists were every bit as keen as their car-driving counterparts to enter into competitions overseas. Here are (left to right) Eric Williams (AJS), Hugh Gibson (Raleigh s/c) and F. Newman (Douglas) in Geneva during the International Six Days, 1920. *(E. Williams)*

G.S. Boston, a keen sporting amateur, is seen here going flat out in the Newcastle hill-climb held on Muggleswick Common in 1921. *(G.S. Boston)*

Seen here as a young man in the grounds of Mear House, Baynhall, Kempsey, Worcestershire, is 'Ferdo' Lea Smith, later Lord Dudley, the 13th Baron, mounted on a very business-like Sunbeam with the Worcestershire number NP 7550. *(Lord Dudley)*

Charles Sgonina from Cardiff was a very able engineer and racing motorcyclist. He developed the Sgonina Special over many years and it is seen here in its final twin-ohc form, some ten years before Norton's famous 'double-knocker' . . .

. . . and opposite, in close-up, we see the overhead camshaft drive. Sgonina had many successes with this very potent bike. *(Mrs C. Sgonina)*

This lady's fashion is typical of the time (*c.* 1927), but although she poses on the pillion of this B.S.A. she more often occupied the sidecar.

Here are two work-a-day rural motorcyclists with their bikes, a Shropshire-registered (NT 1768) Triumph on the left and a BSA on the right. Rig of the day (since they have no sporting pretensions) is a good thick topcoat, a muffler, and the usual flat cap. *(Ludlow Library)*

Here we see the typical sporting motorcyclist of the late 1920s . . . leather coat, beret and a muffler around his neck. His mount is an ohv 2¾hp Humber on the tank of which he has painted his initials. Alas, the name for which the initials stood remains unknown. *(C. Donovan)*

A.R. Abbott had competed very successfully in motorcycle sport before 1914 but turned to cars in the 1920s. He had many successes in trials with a Clyno in which he is seen here in the Land's End Trial in 1925. *(A.R. Abbott)*

Rosedale Abbey Bank in Yorkshire was a formidable hill. This shot from 1927 shows H.W. Milnes in trouble with his Morris Cowley as C. Thackray goes by confidently in his sports Rover 9/20. *(Ilkley & DMC Ltd)*

Alvis cars were frequently to be seen in competition. Here W.G. Nottage brings his 12/50 up Honister Pass in the London–Edinburgh Trial of 1934 to gain a gold medal. *(W.G. Nottage)*

No gold medals for this Alvis tourer taking part in the 1927 London–Land's End Trial. Beggars Roost proved his undoing. The many spectators hang on precariously wherever they can. *(J. Ahern/D. Irvine)*

The MCC's long-distance trials attracted huge entry lists, but this Rolls-Royce Phantom I saloon seems an unlikely contender. R.S. Harrison was its owner. J. Ahern's 3-litre Invicta keeps it company on 25 May 1928. (*J. Ahern/D. Irvine*)

Frazer Nash cars were always in the thick of sporting events such as tough road trials. Here Miss Wilby takes her car through the Women's Automobile & Sports Association (WASA) High Peaks Trial in 1933. (*Mrs A.G. Gripper*)

Again in the WASA High Peaks Trial, this time in 1934, we see a Riley Imp and a Singer Nine coupé on a comparatively easy section. *(Mrs A.G. Gripper)*

Opposite: In the same trial we see Mrs A.G. Gripper at the wheel of a Wolseley Hornet, her husband beside her. This car still survives in appreciative hands. *(Mrs A.G. Gripper)*

A splendid view of the Gripper's Frazer Nash on Park Rash when taking part in the London–Edinburgh Trial in 1932. Despite the remoteness of this area spectators turned out in force. *(Mrs A.G. Gripper)*

J.F.E. Rawlings at the wheel of his MG Magnette taking part in the MCC London–Land's End Trial in 1936, in which he gained a bronze medal. In retirement Rawlings kept a pub in Herefordshire where some of his motoring trophies and photographs were on display. *(J.F.E. Rawlings)*

An Austin 12 of about 1932 is seen here on the way to what would seem to be a singularly desolate camp site. Tent and equipment are on the luggage grid and in the trailer. *(R.A. Bird)*

An Austin 16/6 and a smaller 12/6 both bearing Birmingham numbers, at what appears to be the home of a well-to-do Midlands family.

The Bugatti may not be the latest model but this young 1920s lady looks a happy and contented motorist. *(Pritchard, Hereford)*

This family with their London-registered 1933 Aston Martin 1½-litre saloon halt at a café advertising morning coffee, lunches and teas. *(J. Dearling)*

A high-chassis 4½-litre Invicta is seen in the grounds of Fairmile, Cobham, with Violette Cordery who achieved many long-distance records with Invicta cars. *(C. Cottrell)*

A handsome 30hp Lanchester Straight-8 with saloon coachwork and a Surrey registration finds a shady nook. Clearly visible is Lanchester's characteristic 'porthole', ('scuttle' if you are a sailor) that allows the water level to be instantly established.

Arrol-Aster was a make that came into being through the merger between two old-established makes, Arrol-Johnston of Scotland and Aster of Wembley. Here is one of their very handsome productions.

The Riley 'Imp' and its 6-cylinder sister the 'MPH' were two sporting Rileys with a basically similar rakish body design. This particular car fortunately still survives.

Rather surprisingly, the old-established firm of Vauxhall turned to sleeve valves for their large 25/70 which usually, as here, carried closed coachwork, of which this is a rather sober example.

Here is an attractive blend of quality American chassis, the St-8 Stutz, and bespoke British coachwork.

Auburn was another quality American product. This example wears a saloon body style that became popular in the late 1920s. Even the rather strange design of windscreen wasn't unique to this make.

The Marmon was also one of the better American makes. The author recalls, as a boy of about eight years old, sitting on the driver's lap and steering a similar saloon round the lanes of rural Buckinghamshire. Here the proud owner stands beside an identical Birmingham-registered example.

Another happy marriage between quality American engineering and formal English coachwork, in this case a Packard chassis with sedanca-de-ville coachwork.

This mock-up of Campbell's LSR 'Bluebird' was constructed on a Citroën chassis by Watson's Motor Works for a charity event. *(Watson's Motor Works)*

A reminder that Brooklands was an aviation centre as well as a race track. Here, in the 1933 500-Miles Race, Balmain's MG passes the aftermath of an aviation 'contretemps' around which spectators gather. *(W. Gibbs)*

This 'Parallite' body, Patent no. 410510, was the design of M. Haworth-Booth in the early 1930s. Streamline saloon bodies were fashionable introductions at the time. This design incorporated a full-width body with luggage and locker space within the body. The Wolseley Hornet chassis on which the body is mounted is too small to do the concept justice, but Lancefield built several on larger chassis – Armstrong-Siddeley, Alvis and Hudson. Even so, the public was reluctant to fall in with the idea, and like the better-known Chrysler 'Airflow', it was not a commercial success.

Miss Victoria Worsley was a versatile and experienced motorist who was catholic in her choice of make. Here she has a Jowett smartly turned out for the JCC High Speed Trial at Brooklands, 16 June 1928. (*The Jowett CC*)

C.D. Wallbank bought one of the 1914 TT Humbers after the war and raced it regularly at Brooklands. This shot shows his crowning success when he easily won the 36th 90mph Handicap on 5 August 1929. The car's designer was present and was delighted to see his old car become a winner. Sadly, F.T. Burgess, the designer in question, died shortly afterwards. *(N.W. Portway)*

A charming picture of Woolf Barnato in the 6½-litre Bentley with which he won the 1930 Double-Twelve race at Brooklands at 86.88mph. Beside him is his daughter in a Bentley miniature.

Jack Dunfee with the ex-Campbell Ballot in 1930, when he deliberately lost a duel with Ernie Nott's Rudge motorcycle at a BMCRC Meeting. *(W. Gibbs)*

Here Mrs A.G. Gripper, herself a talented racing-driver, poses beside a splendid D8S Delage at Brooklands Guy's Hospital Charity Event in 1932. *(Mrs A.G. Gripper)*

MGs were very prominent and often successful in various 1930s sporting events. Here an unidentified racing Magnette K3 that has obviously just been stripped of road equipment waits for the action. The car in front is a Ford V8 saloon.

Start of a Mountain Handicap on 13 October 1934. In this varied and busy scene 'Ebby' (E.V. Ebblewhite) in the inevitable Homburg hat has just flagged off no. 7. *(A.B.I. Dick)*

Action in the pits as the Pacey-Hassan of Pacey/Baker-Carr pulls in during the 500-Miles Race, 1936. It finished in second place and was a Gold Star winner in that year. *(D.P Brogden)*

Here is the Hotchkiss driven by Divo/Rose in the 500-Miles Race at Brooklands on 21 September 1935, an unusual visitor. They achieved an average speed of 106.68mph. *(A.B.I. Dick)*

British Empire Trophy, 6 July 1935. Prince von Leiningen's ERA leads E.R. Hall's MG Magnette through the Fork chicane. *(A.B.I. Dick)*

Brooklands, 200-Mile Race, 1925. No. 16 is G.E.T. Eyston's Aston Martin (XR3941). No. 15 is Robert Morgan in his Hooker-Thomas engined ex-Zborowski GP car known as 'Green Pea', and no. 9 is Halford in the first version of his advanced AM-Halford Special. *(M.A. Hill/VSCC)*

1936 was the last year of the Ulster TT on the Ards circuit. Here is the start with, left to right, Embiricos (Bugatti no. 16), Mongin (Delahaye no. 14), Clarke (Delahaye no. 12), Brunet/Martin (Delahaye no. 11) and Lebegue/Mahé (Delahaye no. 10). *(D.P. Brogden)*

The appearance of the German Mercedes-Benz and Auto-Union teams on British soil at Donington Park caused a sensation because of their speed, noise and efficiency. Here is Hesse (Auto-Union) at Melbourne Hairpin. The car is travelling right to left. *(M. Staines)*

Holiday makers at Newquay, 1935, with a Morris Ten-Six Sports registered in Leeds and an MG 14/40 in the foreground.

A 1937 Morris Eight tourer heads into Wales and the hills. Some makers of small cars continued to offer open models until the outbreak of the Second World War.

A sample of London traffic in the late 1930s as Armstrong-Siddeley, Daimler and Rolls-Royce can be distinguished among the numerous taxis.

A Morris Eight Series E tourer that undertook an ambitious Land's End to John O'Groats holiday in the summer of 1939, the year this model was introduced.

This car was extensively used by its Worcester owners in the year before the war. Their travels embraced a trip to John O'Groats and Dornoch Firth, seen here.

Shelsley Walsh achieved international status in 1930, in which year von Stück, the German ace, broke the record for the hill with this Austro-Daimler. *(W. Gibbs)*

Pictures of the finish of the hill are harder to come by than those lower down. In this photograph we see S.H. Newsome's Lea-Francis in 1932. His time was 63.6 seconds for his one run. *(M. Crosthwaite)*

The popularity of Shelsley Walsh is very evident in this shot of L.P. Driscoll with his ohc Austin Seven at the Esses. His times were 45.4 seconds and 43.4 seconds respectively. *(W. Gibbs)*

This Ford Ten tourer, Model 7W, of 1937/8, displays the recently introduced 'L' ('learner') plates that indicated a provisional licence holder. 1,639 of this model were built.

Capt. G.E.T. Eyston was a most versatile driver and broke records galore with many different makes. Here he is at Montlhèry in October 1933 where this busy scene sees him preparing for another attempt on a 24-hour record with a Hotchkiss. Note the lights behind the grille. *(Mrs E. Elwes)*

Freddie Dixon and Cyril Paul share the spoils of success with their Riley in the Mannin Beg in the Isle of Man, 1935. In those days they drank the bubbly!

Above: H.J. Aldington outside the premises of Frazer-Nash Cars with the Bertelli-designed coachwork on a Frazer-Nash-BMW that belonged to Lionel Martin and of which he was very proud . . . (*T. Harding*)

. . . and here is a smiling Lionel Martin being almost swallowed by his car's bonnet at Brooklands. (*Addis/Henley Collection*)

One of the pleasures of the halcyon days was the fact that one could come upon interesting cars quite casually going about their business. Here is a Lagonda Rapier, a beautifully-built 2-ohc sports car capable of a fast and refined performance, pictured in Old Beaconsfield on the A40.

Below: The beautiful workmanship of Vittorio Jano's Type 6C super-sports Alfa Romeo comes under the expert scrutiny of Mr Cottrell, one of Thompson & Taylor's most senior mechanical engineers who travelled all over the world to care for clients' racing cars. *(C. Cottrell)*

A typical late 1930s garage and filling-station much cluttered with advertisements and boasting a lady pump attendant. Look closely, however, and you see Cleveland petrol at 1*s* 3*d* per gallon! Halcyon days indeed!

This is known to be an SS of the pre-Jaguar age though the coachwork is non-standard. Registered in Ayrshire, records no longer exist.

A number of coachbuilders crafted handsome bodywork on the 1930s Lagondas, but few could match the elegance of the 'in-house' product designed by Frank Feeley as this beautifully proportioned dhc 1938 4½-litre LG6 ably demonstrates.

Following the TT tradition of allowing racing to take place over roads closed to the public, the Manx authorities promoted 'round-the-houses' races in Douglas and its immediate environs. Here Cyril Paul in an ERA leads 'B. Bira's' sister car in the RAC International Race on 28 May 1936.

John Cobb, record-breaking at Montlhèry with the big Napier-Railton, receives a pit signal. Fortunately this splendid car still survives. *(C. Cottrell)*

The last of Riley's pre-war models is standing outside Hightree School, Leintwardine, Herefordshire. *(Leintwardine Local History Society)*

Llandudno and Rhyl were very popular tourist resorts. Portrayed here are (left to right) a Wolseley, a Standard Flying Nine and a Hillman Minx, all popular family cars, on the front at Llandudno.

Since its inception, the motor car has always figured in art. Particularly in pre-1914 days, some of the finest motoring posters were produced by leading artists in that genre. Usually they were impressionistic with a fair bit of artistic licence. This example is taken from a Brooklands programme of 1922.

Below: At the other end of the scale was the finely detailed draughtsman's drawing, almost always in side elevation, as here.

The Riley was an old-established and successful make that by 1938 had been acquired by the Nuffield Organisation. Seen here is a 1½-litre saloon of that year, in pristine condition.

The sands of time are running out but the sands at Pendine are full of activity in the beautiful weather of the last pre-war August Bank Holiday. Here is J.D. Barnie with his 490cc International Norton flat along the tank. *(Lynn Hughes)*

Local club events did much to foster enthusiasm and were sometimes the nursery of drivers who later became famous. Here a Sunbeam-Talbot saloon with a Shropshire plate leaves a check point in a narrow lane.

COMPTON. SONS & TERRY.
COACHBUILDERS.

47a High Path,
Merton Road, Merton.
S. Wimbledon.
Mr Arthur P. Compton

PK 7930

1st registered 28.3.1929

This coachbuilder's photograph reached the author nineteen years after he had parted with this very car. It also brought to light the hitherto unknown history of the first four years of the car's life. It is a Super-Sports low-chassis (no. 5) Arab. By the time the author owned it, it was fitted with a stylish open body, this original fhc having been written off in a smash by the car's first owner. *(B.K. Goodman)*

DOC 212

A fine Rover sports saloon, nicknamed from its registration no. 'The Doc', sports an impressive array of horns and lights in this 1937 photograph. *(R.A. Bird)*

This Austin saloon carried a specialist electrical engineer all over the country during the war, often on top-secret assignments, in the course of which he met many of the highest-level service and civilian personnel. The registration is a Herefordshire one. *(J. Page)*

Too old or incapacitated to drive his Armstrong-Siddeley, Daimler or whatever, this elderly gentleman, still sporting his vintage 'flat 'at' (and note the Veteran Motorists 'V' badge mounted up front) is now electrically mobile and has ample time to reflect on the halcyon days of old in which all his motoring had been done.